First Facts®

The Solar System

# Venus

by Adele Richardson

Consultant:
Stephen J. Kortenkamp, PhD
Research Scientist
Planetary Science Institute, Tucson, Arizona

Capstone press®

Mankato, Minnesota

245 4219

First Facts is published by Capstone Press,
151 Good Counsel Drive, P.O. Box 669, Mankato, Minnesota 56002.
www.capstonepress.com

*Library of Congress Cataloging-in-Publication Data*
Richardson, Adele, 1966–
    Venus / by Adele Richardson.—Rev. and updated.
    p. cm.—(First facts. The Solar system)
    Includes bibliographical references and index.
    ISBN-13: 978-1-4296-0729-2 (hardcover : alk. paper)
    ISBN-10: 1-4296-0729-7 (hardcover : alk. paper)
    1. Venus (Planet)—Juvenile literature. I. Title. II. Series.
QB621.R53 2008
523.42—dc22                                                   2007003537

Summary: Discusses the orbit, atmosphere, surface features, and exploration of the
    planet Venus.

**Editorial Credits**
Christopher Harbo, editor; Juliette Peters, designer and illustrator; Jo Miller, photo researcher;
    Scott Thoms, photo editor

**Photo Credits**
Astronomical Society of the Pacific/NASA, 8
European Space Agency, 17
NASA/JPL, 14–15
National Space Science Data Center/NASA, 20
Photodisc, 1, 4, 11, planet images within illustrations and chart, 6, 7, 9, 10, 13, 19, 21
Photo Researchers Inc./Science Photo Library/NASA, cover; Pekka Parviainen, 16
Space Images/NASA/JPL, 5

1 2 3 4 5 6 12 11 10 09 08 07

# Table of Contents

# *Magellan* and Venus

Many spacecraft have visited Venus. In 1990, the *Magellan* spacecraft began circling the planet. *Magellan* used **radar** to make a map of the planet's surface. Scientists learned Venus has a rocky surface with many old volcanoes.

## Fast Facts about Venus

**Diameter:** 7,521 miles (12,104 kilometers)
**Average Distance from Sun:** 67 million miles (108 million kilometers)
**Average Temperature (surface):** 900 degrees Fahrenheit (482 degrees Celsius)
**Length of Rotation:** 243 Earth days
**Length of Day:** 117 Earth days
**Length of Year:** 225 Earth days
**Moons:** None

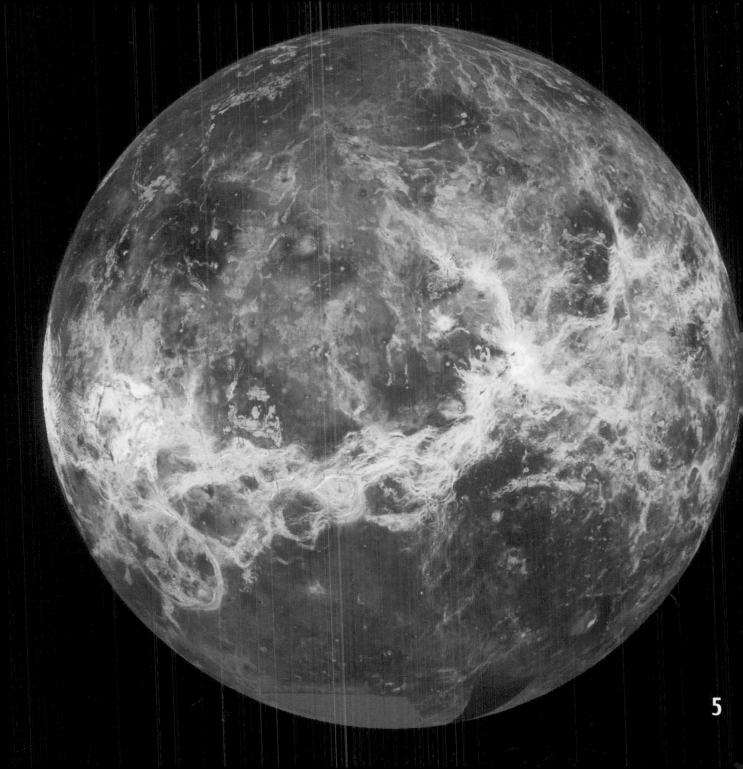

5

# The Solar System

Venus is the second planet from the Sun. Mercury is closer, while Earth and Mars are farther away. These near planets are made of rock. Jupiter, Saturn, Uranus, and Neptune are farther from the Sun. They are made of gases and ice.

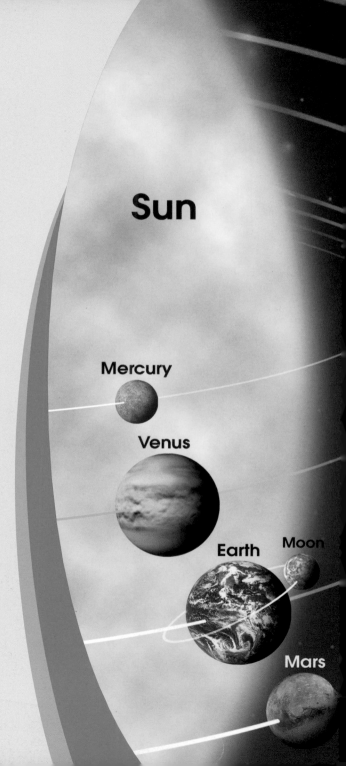

Sun

Mercury

Venus

Earth

Moon

Mars

Jupiter

Saturn

Uranus

Neptune

7

# Venus' Atmosphere

Venus has a very thick **atmosphere**. An atmosphere is the layer of gases that surrounds a planet. Venus is surrounded mostly by **carbon dioxide** gas.

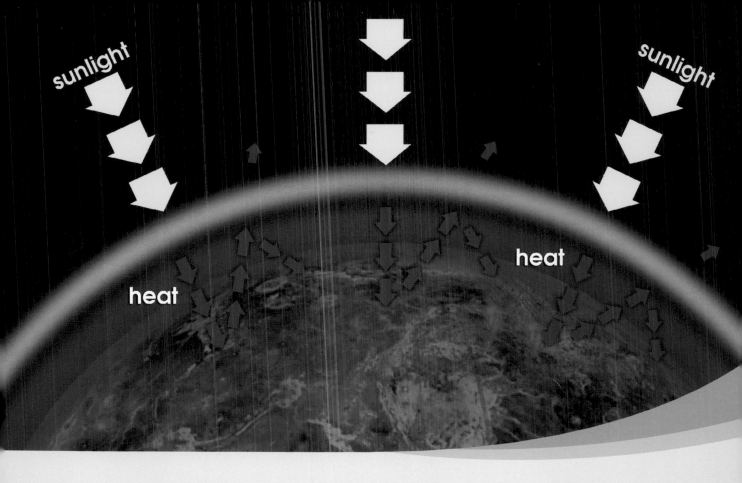

Venus is the hottest planet in the solar system. Venus' thick atmosphere keeps the planet very hot. The atmosphere traps the heat from the Sun.

# Venus' Makeup

Venus' **core** is made of iron and nickel. A rocky **mantle** lies above the core. The surface, or crust, of Venus is made of rock.

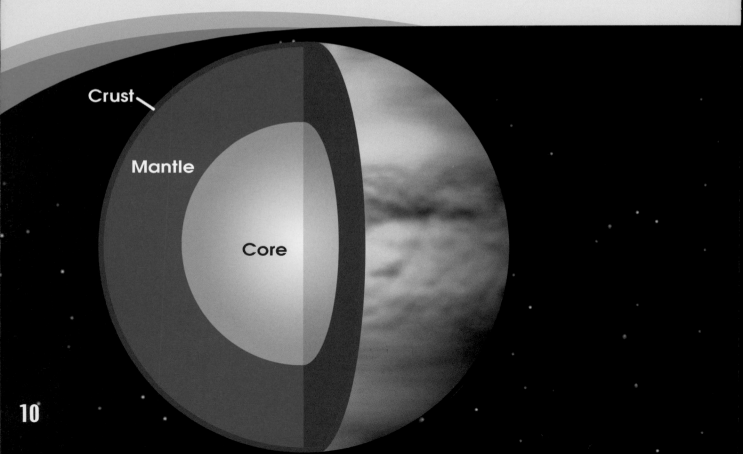

Crust

Mantle

Core

Flat areas and hills cover the surface of Venus. The planet also has mountains, volcanoes, and canyons.

# How Venus Moves

Venus circles around the Sun while it spins on its **axis**. Venus circles the Sun in 225 Earth days. This period of time is one year on Venus. Venus spins on its axis in the opposite direction that Earth spins. Venus takes 243 Earth days to spin on its axis once.

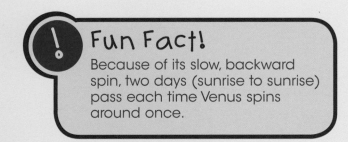

**Fun Fact!**
Because of its slow, backward spin, two days (sunrise to sunrise) pass each time Venus spins around once.

Sun

Venus

Path around the Sun

Axis

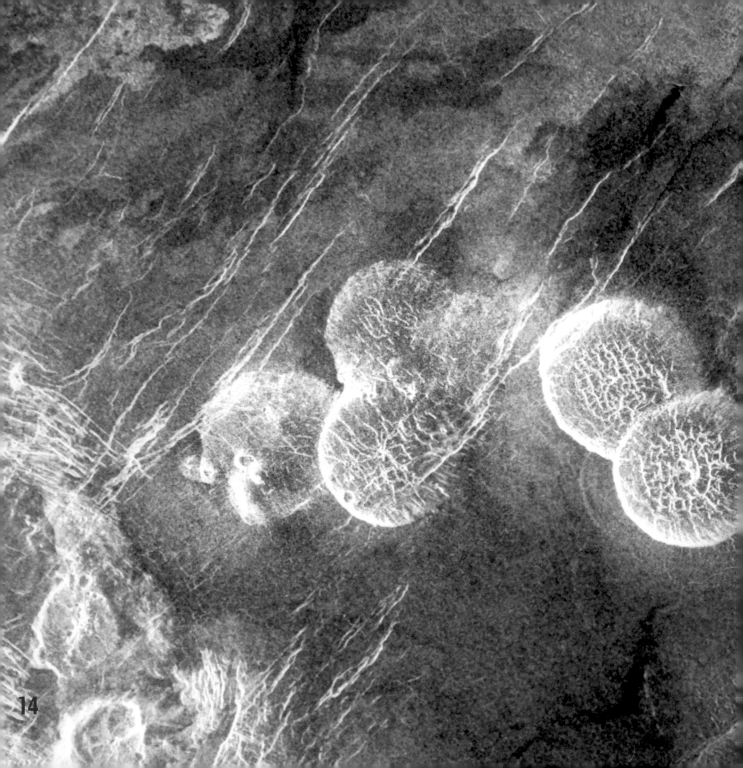

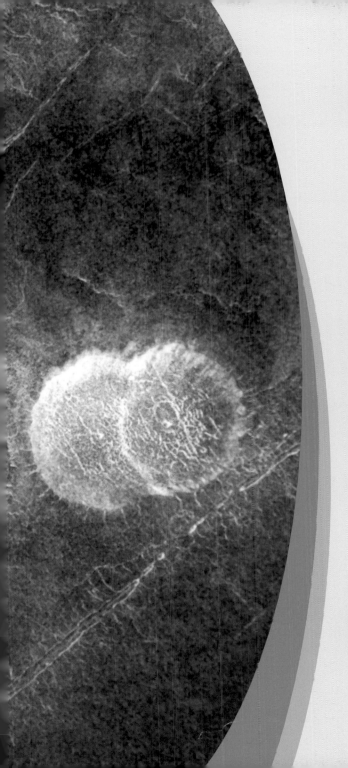

# Pancake Volcanoes

Some volcanoes on Venus have tops that look like pancakes. The tops may have formed from extra thick lava. Some scientists believe the crushing **air pressure** on Venus flattened the tops into pancake shapes.

**Fun Fact!**
Venus' air pressure is 90 times greater than Earth's. It could crush a soda can instantly.

## Studying Venus

Venus is bright in the night sky. The planet is easy to see from Earth. People also use telescopes to get a closer look at the planet.

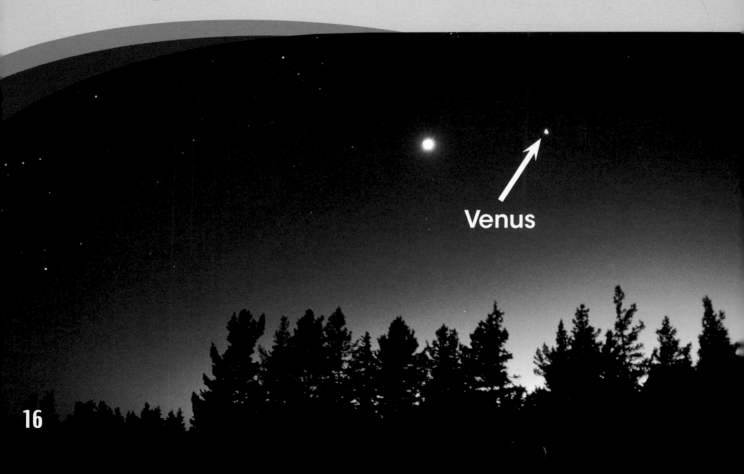

Venus

Scientists study Venus with spacecraft.
In 2005, the European Space Agency sent a
spacecraft to Venus. *Venus Express* studied
the planet's thick atmosphere.

# Comparing Venus to Earth

Venus and Earth are both rocky planets. But Venus is very different. People could not live there. They could not breathe the air. The air pressure on the planet would crush people. The heat would be deadly.

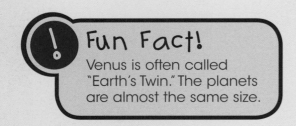

**Fun Fact!**
Venus is often called "Earth's Twin." The planets are almost the same size.

# Size Comparison

Earth

Venus

# Amazing but True!

The first color pictures of Venus' surface were taken in 1982. The Soviet Union's *Venera 13* spacecraft took the pictures when it landed on Venus. These pictures show an orange surface covered with flat rocks.

# Planet Comparison Chart

| Planet | Size Rank (1=largest) | Makeup | 1 Trip around the Sun (Earth Time) |
|---|---|---|---|
| Mercury | 8 | rock | 88 days |
| Venus | 6 | rock | 225 days |
| Earth | 5 | rock | 365 days, 6 hours |
| Mars | 7 | rock | 687 days |
| Jupiter | 1 | gases and ice | 11 years, 11 months |
| Saturn | 2 | gases and ice | 29 years, 6 months |
| Uranus | 3 | gases and ice | 84 years |
| Neptune | 4 | gases and ice | 164 years, 10 months |

# Glossary

**air pressure** (AIR PRESH-ur)—the weight of the air on a surface

**atmosphere** (AT-muhss-feehr)—the mixture of gases that surrounds some planets and moons

**axis** (AK-siss)—an imaginary line that runs through the middle of a planet; a planet spins on its axis.

**carbon dioxide** (KAR-buhn dye-OK-side)—a gas that has no smell or color

**core** (KOR)—the inner part of a planet that is made of metal or rock

**mantle** (MAN-tuhl)—the part of a planet between the crust and the core

**radar** (RAY-dar)—a machine that uses radio waves to locate distant objects

# Read More

**Chrismer, Melanie.** *Venus.* Scholastic News Nonfiction Readers. New York: Children's Press, 2007.

**Dunn, Mary R.** *A Look at Venus.* Astronomy Now. New York: PowerKids Press, 2008.

**Kortenkamp, Steve.** *Why Isn't Pluto a Planet?: A Book about Planets.* First Facts: Why in the World? Mankato, Minn.: Capstone Press, 2007.

# Internet Sites

FactHound offers a safe, fun way to find Internet sites related to this book. All of the sites on FactHound have been researched by our staff.

Here's how:
1. Visit *www.facthound.com*
2. Choose your grade level.
3. Type in this book ID **1429607297** for age-appropriate sites. You may also browse subjects by clicking on letters, or by clicking on pictures and words.
4. Click on the **Fetch It** button.

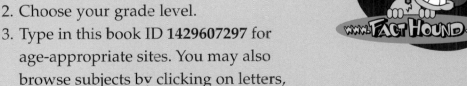

**FactHound will fetch the best sites for you!**

# Index